YOUR GREATEST GIFT

OCT 24, 2021

TO JANE

Hope you ENJOY THIS Book
AS MUCH AS I DID
HAD TO BUY YOU A COPY AS (MY COPY)
IS MARKED UP WITH HIGHLITES

"MAYBE" TOM WILL LIKE IT
AFTER YOU FINISH!

Jim

Your Greatest Gift

That Unlocks All Manifestations

Richard Dotts

© Richard Dotts 2015
1st edition
ISBN-13: 9781517549800
ISBN-10: 1517549809
Questions / comments? The author can be contacted at
RichardDotts@gmail.com

TABLE OF CONTENTS

CHAPTER ONE

YOUR GREATEST GIFT IS WITHIN YOU RIGHT NOW

You have, in your possession right now, the greatest gift you'll ever come into contact with. This gift, when used correctly, will allow you to break through limitations and challenges in your life and steer your life along the course of your wildest dreams. This is the gift that unlocks your deepest desires and brings them into your life in a tangible, physical form. No more just merely wishing for good things to happen. When you correctly utilize the greatest gift that has been bestowed upon you by the Universe, you live with a deep sense of knowingness that good things *will* happen to you. All you have to do is *think* it, and it is done. No matter what you ask for, be it greater happiness, health or wealth, an understanding of this magical gift allows you to enjoy it all.

Why am I so certain that this gift exists in everyone? In my past decade of work as a teacher, entrepreneur and spiritual explorer, I have come into contact with individuals from all walks of life. From spiritual healers and mystics to hard-nosed, weather-beaten businessmen out in the trenches of Wall Street, from the young to the old, I have met them all. In each of these varied encounters, I observed a constant, and it is this: I could see this gift clearly in their eyes. I could see this precious gift right in the very center of their being. Of course, some of their eyes showed signs of betrayal, lost hope and weariness brought on by years of struggle and strain. Some of their bodies showed signs of weakness and physical ailments after years of limited thinking and living. But despite the signs I observed at a physical level, I also saw glimmers of this priceless gift right within them, just waiting to be activated by a chance encounter with a gentle soul.

I have always been sensitive to the feelings of others while growing up as an only child. Not having any siblings to play with and without the luxury of modern technological toys, I often engaged in elaborate make-believe play with my inanimate toys. Unbeknown to me, this resulted in the development of an intricate inner world that I learned to navigate using my inner senses. I could play for hours on end while sitting at the same spot. While I appeared to be doing nothing on the outside, I was actually having a wild adventure on the inside—having ongoing conversations with my imaginary friends and partaking in their wonderful worlds. How did my young, barely educated mind know how to come up with such wonderfully complex inner worlds when it did not have anything to reference? How does a young child know what to create?

As I revisit these topics several decades later as a researcher in the field of behavioral psychology, I find myself becoming increasingly frustrated that science does not have all the answers. The existing models of science are severely limited in their approach. One has to understand that even when conducting cutting-edge high-level research, existing theories are used as frameworks to formulate possible hypotheses. The use of existing theories to guide predictions has already restricted and set up certain "expectations" for the researcher. As such, unexpected results are often dismissed as erratic, with the data ignored and studies rerun *until* the results turn up as hypothesized. At other times, researchers deliberately seek surprising" results in the hopes of getting published in top journals. This means going to great lengths to design studies that solicit those surprising results and ignoring research in more fundamental areas. Either way, it shows that scientific research is not really as self-directed and independent as it seems.

While I may seem to be criticizing the scientific method, I am actually not as opposed to it as other New Age teachers and writers, many of whom have made the transition from fully scientific empirical research to more anecdotal approaches. I believe that striking a balance is important and the key lies in recognizing the boundaries of current scientific research. There are answers that science is very good at eliciting and there are many areas where rigorous empirical research can be put to good use. However, there are also many questions that science cannot answer, for which we have to use a more spiritual or metaphysical approach. Knowing when to use which approach, and when to blend two approaches such that they become complementary or even synergistic, is of great value to a practitioner.

For this reason, I thank my scientific mind for helping me achieve several breakthroughs in the spiritual realm and arrive at several ah-ha moments. But I also note that my scientific mind has held me back and limited me at other times when I tried to apply some spiritual principles. It was only when I learned to use both approaches cooperatively that I achieved the best results.

Back to the earlier question: How does a child know what to create? Think back to the time when you were a young child. You just played for hours on end, fascinated by everything you created in your inner world and aided by the physical world around you. I am sure many of us can vividly remember talking to our imaginary friends and making up imaginary conversations. We flitted effortlessly from one topic to the next, from one segment to the next. We could have been playing in a dark castle in one moment and a park on a rainy day in the next. Scientific theory would attribute these mental creations to an overly active imagination, but it does not explain the exact inner workings of the brain. How do young children, not educated in the ways of the world, know how to create so effortlessly? How do they come up with all the mental imagery and make them real? Why do they believe fully in what they creates? Can they turn their inner creations into tangible, physical reality?

Spiritual healers have often cited a sense of childlike wonder as a necessary ingredient for any kind of spiritual healing work. Similarly, I have written about the importance of quieting the reasoning, judgmental mind when doing this inner work. We will touch on these topics in greater detail as the book progresses. But for now, it is interesting to ponder how we are all born creators at heart, with the infinite potential to create whatever we want in our lives. More importantly, we were all born *without* that sense of judgment, where we could just freely perceive the world around us with love and kindness. These abilities are still latent within us today; it is just that they have been overridden by more conventional schooling and the societal conditioning that we subsequently received.

I remember being suddenly gripped by strong emotions when I came into the presence of others. It took me several decades to realize that I was actually picking up on the deepest feelings of those around me. Sometimes this resulted in a mishmash of chaotic feelings and emotions, some of them my own and some picked up from those around me. Since most people walk around with a sense of worry and fear about the future, it wasn't surprising that the feeling I picked up on the most often was that of fear. As a result, I became a very timid child who preferred to spend my time alone. I did not understand that the feelings I felt were not my own, but were picked up from the energetic field around me. As a child, I really had nothing in my life to be afraid of.

As I grew out of my extreme timidity over the years, I also lost much of my ability to pick up on the feelings of others around me. I became caught up on the same treadmill of career advancement as all the others before me, striving and working very hard in the outer world. Despite trying very hard and doing everything I could to get ahead in society, I sensed a growing inner dissatisfaction that gnawed at my heart. "There has to be something more to life than this," I frequently thought to myself. I was determined to find out what that missing element was, and thus set out on a journey to read all the self-help and personal development books I could get my hands on. This marked the start of my journey.

Years later, even after a career as a business owner and teacher, I never gave up on the inner work, which I continued to do on the side. I saw my "sideline work" as an integral part of my life. It was more than a hobby. I had always intuitively known that if I was going to transform my life for the better, then this change had to come from the inside.

I looked at several of my well-to-do family members and noticed that while they had all the worldly trappings of success, they were almost never at peace with themselves. They were always highly-strung, constantly criticizing their coworkers, bosses, the government, blaming the economy, worrying about their health or envious about the achievements of others. I had an uncle who was financially rich, but would not allow himself to enjoy a single dollar of his wealth. He lived like a beggar and was plagued with pain in his body. For all intents and purposes, he was living no differently from one. If this is what worldly success meant, I was willing to forgo it!

It is one thing to know that we are blessed with powerful minds, but it is another thing altogether to apply this knowledge in a way that transforms our lives. This is why the greatest quest in my life has been to look for practical methods and solutions where we can express our greatest potential. The scientific method cannot help us to achieve this. It merely deconstructs what is already known for the purpose of studying it. Although we all know that the process of photosynthesis allows a plant to make food and give out oxygen, we have yet to construct an artificial leaf in the lab that can replicate this process of nature. While I am sure this will become a reality in the near future, it shows that man has to take painstaking steps just to recreate what nature can effortlessly do for herself. This is testament to the great divine intelligence that runs through all things in our Universe.

In a similar sense, why not go directly to the source when living our lives? Why not tap into this infinitely powerful source of Universal energy that creates worlds instead of trying to figure out all the petty problems in our lives? Doing so would be like trying to perform mathematical calculations by hand when you have a powerful computer to help you.

Let the Universe do all the work for you as it is meant to, while you sit back and watch with a child-like sense of wonder. When you finally find a way to get in touch with this greatest gift of yours, you'll find worlds and possibilities instantly unlocked. Nothing will ever seem out of reach for you again. You'll know exactly what needs to be done and how to do it. In fact, you will merge and become one with the Universal mind, where all things are possible.

It is my intention to guide you through this process and show you what I have discovered for myself by bridging the gap between theory and practice. I want to show you how I first discovered this greatest gift for myself after dismissing it several times, how I was gently led to it and how I moved from a literal interpretation of this gift into a subtler one that transcends the physical boundaries of space and time that separate us. Finally, it is my greatest wish that you will take this gift out into the world and share it with others by helping them discover this part of themselves that has always existed within their divine nature. I am so excited about this journey we are about to embark on together.

Chapter Two

The Greatest Gift Is Easily Overlooked By Many

Don't worry, I'm not going to tell you that your greatest gift is to be blessed with a powerful mind or that you have the infinitely powerful creative abilities of a manifestor. You already know all that. It is one thing to *know* that you have a powerful subconscious mind at your disposal, but it is another thing altogether to learn how to tap into it. Hundreds of books have already told you the same thing: That you are blessed with the innate abilities of a creator. That you have the ability to dream and achieve those dreams, whatever they may be. That you have deep resources within you to transcend limitations and boundaries. These are concepts that a young child instinctively knows without question, yet we have grown as adults to fervently reject and argue against them.

After burning through hundreds of self-help books in my early days talking about these success principles, I felt no different from when I started. I could repeat all the techniques and teachings verbatim to those around me, but I fell short when trying to apply them to my life. As a result, all of the rich knowledge I accumulated was only on the theoretical level. I could not realize any of those teachings for myself, and any success from trying the techniques was short-lived.

Despite my early failures and disappointments, I always had a deep inkling that this was all supposed to be simple. I always knew that life was not supposed to be complicated and that it would not be difficult to thrive. Matthew 6:28 comes to mind: Consider the lilies of the field, how they grow; they toil not, neither do they spin. God was telling us in parables that the hard work and struggle is always optional. However, my physical experiences at that time contradicted these vague inner knowings. I eventually came to believe in the need for hard work and struggle, just like everyone else. I had unknowingly taken part in the big societal rat race where everyone was running furiously with their eyes closed, not even knowing where they were going or what they were striving for.

This is not a mystery book, so I will reveal the greatest gift to you in a moment. Before I do, however, I would like to set the stage for its revelation. The reason is because the greatest gift does not come in a form that we would expect. Indeed, if we knew what we were looking out for, we would have found this gift long ago. This greatest gift comes in a form that is so unexpected and out of the ordinary that the majority of the population will dismiss it without a second thought. It will seem to be something so trivial, so familiar to each and every one of us that we will not pay any attention to it. Yet I know now, after years of applying this material, that this is the true shortcut. This is the real secret. If there is any "secret" to success, it does not get any closer than this.

What form do you think this greatest gift would come in? Most people readily claim that receiving a huge sum of money would be their greatest gift! Or how receiving the gift of knowledge to solve any problem in life would be the greatest gift to them. Both of these answers reflect the misguided belief pervasive in our society that the most valuable things are those *outside* of ourselves.

Money is something that is external to us, yet it is revered as a powerful problem-solving tool in our modern society. I've heard a famous author teach that if a problem can be solved with money, then it is no longer a problem. Instead, the problem becomes a mere inconvenience! He used this to build a case on why it is important to have money in life.

Of course, this leaves us with all the problems money *cannot* solve and the things money cannot buy. What about issues like health, happiness and relationships? Money is often helpless in such situations, no matter how much of it we have. This is where doing inner spiritual work comes into play. Therefore, if I were to offer a twist on the earlier saying, it would be this: If a problem can be solved spiritually, then it is no longer a problem. It becomes a mere inconvenience!

What problems can be solved spiritually? Since the divine does not even perceive any problems or limitations to begin with, I have found that <u>all</u> problems can be solved spiritually. There is not a single problem or issue in life that cannot be tackled with a spiritual solution. Not a single one, except those that you claim cannot be solved. Once you realize how to bring forth and apply a spiritual solution to every perceived issue in your life, all of these petty issues and concerns automatically fall away; they dissolve of their own accord. The things that bothered you in the past no longer irritate you. You become one and at peace with everything.

So now you know that your greatest gift does not come in the form of material goods. It does not come from a place outside of yourself. It does not come in the form of money or riches. Be thankful that your greatest gift does not come in these forms because that would not provide a lasting solution to the perceived problems in your life! I can't even recall how many times I've dropped to my knees and just *prayed* so hard for money to suddenly appear in my life. "Just give me this $10,000 and I can use it to solve my problem straightaway!" Or "Just give me the money I need to make this physically manifest in my life right now!" There comes a point in every spiritual student's life where they will just break down and ask directly for money…but such beseeching rarely works.

Looking back, I am so thankful that the Universe did not just give me money outright whenever I asked for it. It couldn't, as doing so would have been a violation of these Universal principles. But I am glad the money did not just fall into my lap when I asked for it in the past because it would have meant losing out on the opportunities to realize these authentic teachings for myself. If I had somehow managed to get the money back then, I would have solved that particular problem in my life—but more would certainly recur in the future. Thus anything that is external to ourselves can never be an everlasting solution to any issue.

People often look for the wrong solutions to their issues. In a bid to achieve a permanent solution, they ask for a large sum of money to hoard. Hopefully, this sum of money will tide them over through all their problems now and in the future. But I have learned that our reliance can never be placed on any physical objects that are outside of ourselves. Any stack of money or physical resource, no matter how voluminous, can run out one day. There is a physical limit to how much stuff we can amass. On the other hand, there is no limit to how much spiritual abundance we can have. There is no limit to how much our consciousness can hold or how much divine substance there is. There is unlimited good to go around. When you understand things from this energetic perspective, you'll realize that there is always an unlimited stream of universal energy at your command. There is no such thing as a depletion of this stream, because you can easily and effortlessly call more of it forth when it is required.

Think of a child. Does she ever "run out of" imagination? Does she ever run out of ideas and stories to engage herself with? Does she ever run out of play money? She simply makes some more as it is needed! The young child is a reflection of divine consciousness. A young child knows how to tap into this endless stream of goodness and energy that is available to her. That is why we often describe young children as having boundless energy. When we understand the unlimited nature of energy, then we have to ask ourselves why "mental blocks" and "stagnation" occur so frequently to adults? Why do adults feel that their lives are stuck or that they have run out of ideas? What is it that makes the difference between an adult and a child?

For one, the adult believes in scarcity, the child does not. Observe young children playing and you will see that they do not even perceive the concept of scarcity. It just does not exist in their world! Lack is nowhere to be found in their vocabulary. If we adopted this way of thinking and acting in the world and transposed it into our adult minds, what do you think would happen? Would we all start running into problems, spending more than we have—or would we create a new flourishing, a new age of abundance for ourselves? Do not be so quick to answer, instead, just ponder the possibilities.

If we truly took our deep-seated beliefs in lack, scarcity and limitation out of our vocabulary, what do you think would happen? The first tendency is to believe that we would all go amok with our spending and max out all our credit cards, but probe a little deeper and you'll realize that answer to be also one that is rooted in the fear of lack. If lack and limitation were truly eliminated from our belief system, we would all perceive infinite abundance everywhere we turned. There would be no hoarding, no manipulative competition, no rushing to get the things we wanted once we had the money. Therefore, the impulse to spend recklessly only results when we believe in scarcity, but not when we rest in the assurance of complete abundance.

Another question that commonly arises is, "What happens if I'm the odd one out?" What happens if I am the only one in my social circle practicing these spiritual principles, while the people around me (including my family and coworkers) continue to believe in lack and limitation? Wouldn't I be subject to their cutthroat actions while being powerless to defend myself? Once again, I invite you to ponder this statement and the underlying belief. When does one need to defend himself? Only when he perceives a lack of something or a scarce resource. The need to defend oneself only arises when there is a corresponding belief in the lack of something. When you bring forth your greatest gift and apply the spiritual solution to any problem, there is nothing left for you to defend. Others can take as much of what they want from you but you will never be taken advantage of.

Everything will be handled with divine timing and wisdom.

Now all of these realizations did not come to me easily. As mentioned, I was in the corporate rat race for many years, trying to survive and achieve happiness in this world. Yet with every shiny trophy or gadget I collected, I felt a little part of me dying. It felt as if I was selling myself out. Do we really have to sell ourselves out in order to make it in life, or is there an easier way? I kept believing in the existence of an easier way, which is why I never gave up on my study of esoteric materials. I believed that any guidance pertaining to this easier way would not be found in the vast scientific achievements and generated knowledge of mankind, but should instead be something more fundamental. It should be something so obvious that it can be called upon by any man at any time. It should not be a procedure that requires an instruction manual to operate. As it turns out, I was right.

CHAPTER THREE
HOW I DISCOVERED THE GREATEST GIFT FOR MYSELF

As I look back at my life, I can pinpoint two specific incidents that pointed me toward my greatest gift. I also realize that these two incidents were great gifts in themselves, in that they planted in me the seeds for my eventual awakening.

The first incident occurred during my early days as an entrepreneur. I had tried everything possible and was down to the last few hundred dollars in my bank account. All viable income streams seem to have dried up. No clients were knocking on my door and whatever marketing efforts I financed brought zero results. As my mind drifted off to all the financial obligations I had committed to and would have to meet in the following months, a sick feeling of worry welled up in my gut along with a real sense of panic. I had never felt this scared about my finances in my life before.

In times like this, I usually try to take my mind off the subject by reading some of my favorite books. One book I read at that time was "The Nature of Personal Reality" by Jane Roberts. I'll never forget the surreal feeling of calm and comfort that over-came me as I read these two statements by Seth, as channeled by Jane Roberts: (1) Your point of power is in the present. (2) You create your own reality, there is no other way.

I don't know what it is about those words that brought so much faith and peace to my heart. I only know that I felt a real sense of relief after reading those words, and it was relief I'd not experienced in the past few months of sleepless nights. As I pondered those words and read them over and over again, I felt something shift inside me. It was as if I had reached the tipping point for all my worries and now the tides were finally turning in my favor. I still remember excitedly typing out those two statements on a card and pasting them on the wall in front of me. Somehow, an inner sense of calmness and peace overcame me each time I pondered the deeper significance of those words.

The second incident happened shortly after I separated from my business partner. We had parted on unfriendly terms and the business that I inherited was in debt and on the brink of collapse. Yet it was my only viable source of income at that time. We had spent much time building up the business and I was not ready to give it up just yet. However, the reality was that I had only enough money in the bank for no more than three months of living expenses. Those feelings of extreme worry and that sick feeling in my gut started welling up once again. I remember driving around in my beautiful car and wondering how I was going to make ends meet. One day, as I drove my mom around, I casually shared with her some of the concerns that were in my mind at that time: How was I going to keep the business running? How was I going to make ends meet? How was I going to repay the debt from the business?

My mom's answer shocked me and I still remember it to this day. Although she has always been quite the compulsive worrier, she said simply, "I'm sure you will manage this situation. You have always done it in the past and I am confident of your abilities this time round."

I don't know what compelled my mom to speak those words, but it was truly out of character for her. Not only did she *not* worry about the situation, she expressed a deep sense of genuine faith and confidence in me that came right from her heart. She was saying those words not just to comfort me, but because she genuinely believed that I could turn the situation around. Upon hearing her words, I experienced the same sense of calmness and peace that overcame me as I read Seth's words several years earlier. This brought a huge sense of relief and gave me the energy I needed to reorganize my affairs.

Today, I am happy to report that both Seth and my mom were absolutely right. I was indeed in total control of the situation no matter how bleak everything seemed at that time. In fact, shortly after I encountered Seth's words and my mom's comments, things began to turn around for me. I began to find capable individuals who could take over the responsibilities of my ex-business partner. The clients we worked with in the past called and offered us jobs. I was eventually able to pay off our corporate debts in full and turn in a handsome profit for myself as sole owner of the business, double what I would have received in the past. Because I had to run the business on my own, I engineered various ways that allowed our processes to be more efficient, which brought about more gains for the company.

Throughout all the events that transpired, I never once attributed the quick turnaround of the situation to the unconscious application of my greatest gift. I had always assumed that it was some kind of good fortune or some kind of turning of the tides that had occurred. But as I have written several times, there are no coincidences in your life. Everything is in your life for a reason, whether brought about by you or to lead you toward your greater good.

The final guidepost came in the form of a strange inner nudging. I had always felt a strange inner calling to go off to a quiet place in nature and just spend some time by myself. This inner tugging became more intense during times of extreme turmoil and worry on the outside. I observed that whenever I experienced periods of great uncertainty in my life, I would be called upon, as if by some unseen forces of nature, to spend some time alone. There would be an inexplicable urge to spend an afternoon by myself in the park or just take a stroll by the beach. For the longest time, I could never understand why

I felt those sudden compulsions. I had never been a nature lover before, and yet here I was feeling so compelled to spend time in nature!

The significance of all these incidents and nudges did not become clear to me until I started doing the inner work that I advocate across all my books. As I dropped my negative feelings and thought habits, I freed up more of my consciousness to see the general patterns that had always recurred in my life. It was only then that I became truly awakened to all the possibilities. Please know that there is no substitute for doing the inner work necessary. Manifestations and creating your desired reality are not about the piecemeal application of one or two temporary techniques. It is about having such a complete understanding of the material that you are immersed in an inner state conducive for magic and miracles all the time.

As I came to discover what this greatest gift is, I realized several things. First, that the greatest gift is *truly* within each and every one of us. It requires no special training, no special abilities and no superior intellect to operate. Anyone can get in touch with and utilize this greatest gift at any point in their lives. In fact, one may even argue that the "less educated" a person is, the easier it is for him to use this greatest gift that has been bestowed upon him. Second, calling upon the greatest gift is a fundamental ability that each of us has. It is such a basic act that most of us do not even give it a second thought. We just do it without even thinking about it! Therefore, applying the greatest gift is what I call a *thoughtless* activity. There is no thinking involved. There is no need to rationalize, reason or understand *why* you are doing something. No logical thought is needed to apply the greatest gift.

As I made these realizations, I became aware that I had indeed found the easier way that I was looking for so many years ago. There was indeed an easier way and it was staring me right in the face all along. I was being called to it all along. It was just so painfully obvious that I did not recognize it as being so important at first glance.

In fact, I'm going to prove this to you right now. Think about the three events that I described earlier in this chapter. The greatest gift manifests itself as a common thread in each of the three instances above. Before turning the page and reading ahead, make a guess as to what this greatest gift is. What is the gift that was so subtly revealed to me? I can assure you that it is none of the obvious: It is not about the use of affirmations, feeling good, about having faith in oneself or in the Universe, or about spending some time alone to listen for answers within. The greatest gift that is present in each of the three episodes described above is way more fundamental than that. It is such a fundamental action that *anyone* can do it right now, right at this very moment.

Before I understood what the greatest gift was for myself, I used to think that my good only came to me when I went to a certain physical location or place. I came to believe that perhaps being close to nature was good for me because there was positive energy to be found in nature. I also believed that I had to engage in certain rituals in order to attract greater good into my life. After I understood what the greatest gift was, I came to realize that none of this matters. We have been bestowed with such a remarkably simple fundamental knowing, that if applied properly, will catapult us toward our desires in a shorter time than before.

So for now, without turning the page and getting ahead of yourself, just make a guess as to what this greatest gift is. What do you think is this gift that unlocks all manifestations? Even if you have no idea, I would like you to make a wild guess because whatever answer you give can actually turn out to be useful later on in the process. The answer you give is a powerful tool to uncover hidden beliefs and resistances to the manifestation process that are holding you back. This insight, when coupled with your understanding of the greatest gift, will provide you with the unique perspective needed to make this work in the right way for you.

And whenever you're ready, imagine yourself holding on to this exquisite, nicely wrapped cosmic present that holds the keys to all your future dreams and desires. This present is in your hands right now. You just have to turn the page and unwrap the gift to reveal its truest and purest form. Just what form will this generous gift from the Universe take? Will it be in the form of an affirmation, mantra, prayer, chant or none of the above? Will it be an object that you'll actually use for yourself? Will it be some secret, esoteric knowledge? I can assure you that the greatest gift is something simpler than that. So simple in fact, that I had this key in my pocket all the time without realizing all I had to do was to turn it.

CHAPTER FOUR

UNWRAPPING YOUR GREATEST GIFT

What do Seth's words, the encouragement from my mom and sitting quietly by myself in nature have in common? The answer to this question points the way toward the greatest gift that unlocks all manifestations. Not just *my* greatest gift, but yours as well, and that of every single person living on this planet.

Why am I so sure? Ever since I realized the infinite potential of this greatest gift, I have made a conscious decision to apply and bring forth its greatness on a daily basis, at least once a day. My life has never been the same since I actively accessed this gift that has always been inherent in me. But until I made an attempt to bring it forth, this ability lay dormant within me, waiting to be awakened at a moment's notice.

I will first summarize the essence of the greatest gift in one single sentence before explaining further: **Your greatest gift is the sacred feeling of inner peace.** More specifically, it is your ability to access this deep feeling of inner peace at *any* point in your life, no matter where you are or what your outer circumstances may be.

The ability to *feel* a deep, profound sense of inner peace at any moment is a fundamental tenet of *all* the world's major religions, with not a single exception. Ever since discovering this greatest gift for myself, I have seen it appear over and over again in the teachings of the Bible, Dead Sea Scrolls, Tao Te Ching, Buddhist scriptures and so on. Yet somewhat unfortunately, this basic fundamental teaching has been glossed over by modern truth seekers in favor of more complex rituals and spiritual practices. In all of the spiritual practices that are known to be effective and across all the cases of miracles that have been performed, there is always an unchanging constant, and it is **peace**. When I read Seth's words and heard my mom's, this same element was present. Those soothing words brought instant peace to my troubled heart. When I was nudged to take a quiet walk in nature away from all my worldly affairs, the Universe was actually gently nudging me toward **peace**.

Somehow, the infinite intelligence of the Universe knew that if I found some peace within myself, then all the perceived problems in my world would automatically straighten themselves out and drop away. Each time I accessed a bit of that peace for myself, even for just a split second, it created a much-needed opening for the Universe to work its magic and deliver my greater good to me. If I managed to stay with that peace for longer and longer periods of time, I observed that good things would quickly manifest themselves in my physical reality. Therefore, if we want to truly understand the art of manifestations, we have to understand how to access this profound sense of inner peace.

The ability to *feel* a sense of inner peace is our basic nature. It is so fundamental to each and every one of us that we may have dismissed this ability a long time ago. "So what? It's just a feeling of peace" is what many people tend to say. I used to dismiss it too, thinking that *feeling* peaceful on the inside was deluding myself and escaping from all the problems of the real world. But it is no accident that my outer situation began to turn itself around each time I accessed my feelings of inner peace, even for very short periods of time. I have found that how long you stay in a state of peace does not matter. What matters is how *deeply* you access this state of inner peace. The deeper the state, the more profound the outer transformations.

You'll quickly realize that all the spiritual teachings in the world today are built upon the foundation of peace. Without peace, nothing is possible. The practitioner must first bring himself to a place of calmness and peace within before physical transformations can happen on the outside. Therefore, is it possible that this <u>feeling of peace</u> is what causes all the magic and miracles to happen in the first place? Is it possible that this inner peace is the catalyst for all the transformations, rather than the rituals, words, prayers or actions that follow? I think this peace is a necessary condition for all miracles to take place. When you first access that place of peace within yourself, you bring forth latent abilities and potentials to work miracles that have never been used before. You transcend your perceived physical boundaries to become spaceless and timeless.

The first step to utilizing this greatest gift is to get in touch with it as soon as possible. As you do so in the beginning, seek not to immerse yourself in this peace for extended periods of time, but instead to connect with this peace *deeply* and profoundly. Seek a deep connection with this inner peace. If you manage to do so, then even a few seconds fully immersed in peace is sufficient to cause outer shifts in your physical world. Why is getting in touch with this inner sense of peace so important? I have never explained this subject in this manner before, but some groundwork is in order before we move on to the subtler aspects.

The essence of inner peace is a state of **zero.** As I have written in the past, a state of zero is an extremely conducive state for our outer manifestations because we completely drop all negative feelings from our consciousness. However, what I have not emphasized as heavily is that a state of **zero** is also <u>completely</u> neutral. This means one does not feel any positive emotions either. The state of peace is one in which we feel neither positive nor negative. We are completely at rest, at zero. It is a state marked by the conspicuous absence of all of our negative feelings. Fear, worry, desperation, attachment, guilt, irritation, anger and jealously simply do not exist when we achieve that feeling of peace within. At the same time, we hold on to none of the positive emotions, even the supposedly good ones. We let all our positive feelings of joy and happiness go, regardless of how good they may feel to us. The willingness to let go of our good feelings is what will bring us to a state of peace and zero.

For the longest time, I struggled to find the right physical words to explain what happens when we reach a state of complete zero. I had experienced this state for myself over and over again, but was at a loss for words to describe my experience. I wanted to capture the exact essence of what happened when I finally reached that zero-point, but all I could describe were the feelings of deep joy and unconditional love that followed shortly after. As it turns out, bringing oneself to that inner point of peace will automatically result in spontaneous feelings of joy and love. But those feelings are not the feelings of being in a state of complete peace.

It turns out that the words I needed were filled in by quantum physics. I am not saying that this is the last word on the matter, but it is one of those cases where science supplements spirituality beautifully by providing us with a framework with which to understand the material. However, know that your understanding is never a hindrance to your application. You can benefit from all this even without a scientific understanding of the process, in the same way you can flip on a light switch without under-standing the underlying circuitry.

In her excellent book on developing one's intuition titled "Your Sixth Sense," psychotherapist Belleruth Naparstek describes the pendulum theory put forth by Israeli-American scientist and mystic Itzhak Bentov. The late Bentov, known for his stud-ies on consciousness, proposed that since our bod-ies are all made up of energetic particles that are constantly in motion, the back and forth vibrations of each particle follow the swinging motion of a pendulum.

Picture a pendulum swinging from side to side. As it reaches its highest point on either side, the pendulum is in a momentary state of complete rest before making its return journey. According to Bentov, this is when it enters into a zero-point for a very short period of time and becomes nonmaterial in our space-time reality. In that fleeting instance of being at rest, the pendulum actually achieves infinite velocity and is simultaneously present in multiple dimensions of our Universe. However, the moment it resumes its motion, the pendulum once again becomes "present" and rejoins our three-dimensional space-time reality.

Bentov's pendulum offers a fascinating frame-work to interpret the benefits of bringing ourselves to a momentary state of peace even for a split-second. While the pendulum or energetic particle looks completely still, it is actually in such a profound state of stillness that it has gone out of this world into other dimensions. Bentov goes on to assert that our bodies "blink off and on" in this manner at least fourteen times every second, during which we access other dimensions and realities. This is one of the possible channels through which we receive pieces of information not known to us through our five senses.

When I read the description of Bentov's pendulum, I immediately thought about the teachings of Bashar (as channeled by Darryl Anka). Bashar famously said that "when it *seems* like there are no options available to you, that is when there are actually *infinite* options available." I saw the parallels between Bashar's words and Bentov's pendulum almost immediately: While it seems as if the pendulum is doing nothing (at a state of complete rest), it is actually doing and becoming *everything* all at once. It is in such a state of profound stillness that it transcends the space-time limitations of our three-dimensional Universe and achieves a state of omnipotence. No wonder the Universe kept nudging me to find that stillness within myself!

As I think back to the three episodes outlined in the previous chapter, I realize that each of those three instances allowed me to momentarily achieve that state of inner peace. My mind was fraught with worry and fear over my financial future, but reading Seth's words stopped all of those worrisome thoughts and put me in a state of profound peace—even for just a split-second before my worrying resumed again. It was that momentous state of profound peace that I had unknowingly reached that reversed my fortunes.

Subsequently, the same thing happened when I heard the encouraging words from my mom. After losing sleep and spending every single waking moment immersed in my perceived problems at that time, the words from my mom brought a welcome sense of peace and assurance into my life. It did not even matter whether I consciously believed in her words, but those words were all that was needed to create a momentary pause in my chaotic inner thoughts. That pause was all that was needed. In that moment when my inner thoughts came to a complete standstill, I reached that elusive state of *zero*. I had passed through the zero-point where I ever so briefly went "out of this world," became infinite and popped back again.

Did I gain access to pieces of information from other dimensions that somehow led to my subsequent transformations in this world? Or did I manage to tap into powerful Universal forces that were in those dimensions? I will never know for sure, but physical transformations *did* occur for me and Bentov's pendulum is a fascinating possibility to ponder.

As I write this, I am reminded of the two-point technique taught in Matrix Energetics, another spiritual healing modality known for its instantaneous results. The two-point has been attributed to ancient spiritual shamans who practiced it throughout the ages. To those familiar with the technique, the two-point is essentially a method of accessing that inner peace within the healer and the healed. When one applies the two-point technique, he experiences a brief wave of profound peace wash over him, in which the mind goes blank momentarily. When I tried the two-point technique on myself, I experienced a split-second of phasing out, accompanied by a sensation of losing my balance and the motion of falling forward or backward. This description fits surprisingly well with what we have just discussed. In fact, many who have experienced radical physical shifts through the two-point technique describe a feeling of going "out of this world" at the exact moment the technique was applied, while struggling to find exact words to describe the transformations that occurred. This is in line with our limitations and inability to make sense of information from other dimensions.

Whatever the underlying mechanisms may be, nothing beats an actual experience of this gift, so let's get in touch with it right now.

Chapter Five

Experiencing The Greatest Gift For Yourself

Your greatest gift is the ability to connect with and *be* in a state of deep inner peace. While everyone has this ability inherent within themselves, the majority of people readily dismiss it because these feelings come to them so easily. We have no trouble feeling happy one moment and sad or angry the next. Hence most of us consider our feelings as something extraneous, just as sensations that we feel on the inside. What we do not realize is that our feelings influence our inner states and eventually go on to affect our outer manifestations. Put simply, our inner feelings lead to tangible physical manifestations!

A sense of peace is different from a mere feeling. When we *feel* happy, we hold on to the sensations of happiness. In turn, this sense of happiness produces a unique sensation within our bodies that we come to recognize as a happy feeling. Similarly, when we feel angry, our bodies react and respond in a certain way to produce angry sensations, which we also come to recognize as angry feelings. Scientific research has long established that these sensations go beyond just mere fleeting feelings in our body. When held for even short periods of time, our feelings produce actual chemical and biological changes in our body that have an effect on our physical well-being.

While I speak of the "feeling" of peace, I would like to emphasize that peace is not really a "feeling" in the traditional sense of the word. While you may *feel* peaceful, the feeling of peace is characterized by the conspicuous <u>absence</u> of all extraneous feelings and emotions rather than the presence of them. Therefore, the feeling of peace is really the absence of all emotions. This is key to getting in touch with that inner feeling of peace. Many people work very hard at *trying* to feel peaceful, equating a feeling of inner peace with a feeling of happiness. But what I am referring to here goes deeper than that: A deep feeling of inner peace represents the <u>absence</u> of all feelings and emotions, whether they are positive or negative. It is a feelingless state.

As an example, while the inner state of an individual who feels joyful carries a positive charge, this individual is not connecting with that deep sense of inner peace within. Only when he drops those positive feelings of joy will he return to a truly peaceful state. The same applies for an individual holding on to negative feelings.

This is a counterintuitive point that raises several questions. It is easy to see why we should let our negative feelings go, but why would anyone want to drop their positive feelings? Why would someone want to stop feeling good? Aren't our good feelings something to be desired in all of these spiritual teachings?

Indeed, all of the major Law of Attraction teachings out there talk about the importance of feeling good. I have written extensively about how when we feel good, these good feelings go on to attract more good things, people and circumstances in our outer reality that reinforce these good feelings. Therefore, as compared to feeling bad (which leads to undesired manifestations in our outer world), feeling good is something to be desired.

However, in many cases, feeling good also signifies a certain unconscious attachment to the outcome. We feel good because we want good things to happen to us. We feel good because we want to control the outcome. There is also an attachment to the good feelings themselves. This attachment can often be seen in the behavior of metaphysical students, who go to great lengths to avoid any kind of negative feelings for fear that bad things will happen in their lives. This is a subtle attachment to our manifestation outcomes.

The late Lester Levenson, creator of the Sedona Method, talks about being in exalted states of joy that were so intense that he could not sleep for days on end and had to take long walks just to shake off some of that buzzing energy. It wasn't until he made a conscious decision to move from a positive state of joy to a neutral state of peace that he could again function "normally" in the world.

A person who holds on to strong positive feelings on the inside is like an upward swinging pendulum. While there is momentum associated with these positive feelings, he is constantly moving *toward* something and therefore not in a state of peace. Similarly, a person who holds on to strong negative feelings is like a pendulum on its downward swing. He is negatively creating his outer reality by virtue of his negative emotions. Finally, a person who is in a state of profound, inner peace (just like Lester Levenson consciously decided to be) is like that pendulum at the highest point of its path. It becomes out of this world. It is *in* this world but not *of* it. When this happens, the absence of all emotions brings us back to a state of zero and allows us to recognize our true nature, which would otherwise be obscured by all the emotions and feelings that color our inner state.

Putting on a pair of rose tinted shades may make you feel comfortable, but you ultimately know that the "reality" that you perceive through the shades are not real. The same goes with positive feelings held in the pursuit of something. They may make you feel good, but those good feelings that you hold keep you away from recognizing your basic nature. Of course, in between feeling good and feeling bad, you should always choose to feel good. However, if you have progressed past this stage of the teachings and have no trouble feeling blissful most of the time, then you should make a conscious decision to move into a state of inner peace. Between feeling good and peace, you should choose peace.

The state of inner peace is a profound, transformative state that is not often experienced by many. This is not because it takes a special ability to *feel* a sense of deep inner peace, but because there is nothing to be felt at all! We are therefore going after the *absence* of feelings as opposed to the presence of them. Furthermore, the inner states of most individuals are clouded with thoughts and feelings of all kinds. This mind chatter goes on day after day, which makes it difficult for anyone to perceive what underlies all that mind chatter. Think of all your extraneous thoughts and feelings as the scribbles on a piece of paper. When a white piece of paper is filled with so many drawings and scribbles, the piece of paper looks entirely black with not a patch of white space to be seen! This is what most of our inner states look like. Therefore, the goal of these exercises is to reconnect with a piece of the whiteness that has always been there.

Different healing modalities make use of different ways to get in touch with this inner peace. I find it particularly noteworthy that the Bible does not speak as much of happiness, but speaks more of peace. Even then, joy and peace are often mentioned in the same sentence. While I am not a biblical scholar, even casual references to the Bible allow us to identify many sayings related to an inner state of peace. Could there be a deeper significance in these sayings?

In John 20:21, Jesus said, "<u>Peace</u> be with you! As the Father has sent me, I am sending you." In John 14:27, "<u>Peace</u> I leave with you; My <u>peace</u> I give to you; not as the world gives do I give to you. Do not let your heart be troubled, nor let it be fearful."

What is interesting about these scriptures is that Jesus seems to be referring to "peace" as some sort of a *gift* that can be transferred. He first talks about leaving his peace with one person and giving his peace to another person. Then he follows that up with advice on how one should not let oneself feel negative emotions of worry or fear. This is in contrast with our modern day perspective, in which we feel peaceful as a result of stopping our worrisome thoughts. But here, peace is first *given* to the individual, who is then advised to stop engaging in worrisome thoughts.

The Hawaiian spiritual healing tradition of Hooponopono has a beautiful prayer known as the Peace of "I" prayer. Part of the prayer reads:

My Peace "I" give to you,
My Peace "I" leave with you,
Not the world's Peace, but, only My Peace,
The Peace of "I".

Once again, this moving prayer talks about leaving a piece of your peace with another individual, and gifting it from the healer to the healed. This prayer and the biblical references have had a deep impact on me along my spiritual journey. They became my catalysts for exploring the deeper significance of inner peace and how it relates to my outer manifestations.

The more I practiced and researched, the more I realized that spiritual masters and healers over the ages recognized the paramount importance of this inner peace. This peace is a fundamental foundation, a prerequisite that has to be there before seeming miracles can be achieved. When modern day spiritual healers are asked about what goes on in their heads during a healing process, they often reply that they still their minds and stop all conscious thought in order to let some "higher power" direct the healing. Is this why spiritual healers are able to tap into extraordinary healing abilities while in this state? One common characteristic is that these individuals have all found unique ways to get in touch with their inner peace for prolonged periods of time.

Even the practice of applied kinesiology (muscle testing) requires the suspension of all judgment and rational thought in the split-second that the testing is done. This is akin to connecting with that state of inner peace for just a split-second in order to get the answers required.

The final piece of the puzzle came from the late Dr. David Hawkins, an adventurous spiritual teacher who wrote the controversial bestseller "Power vs. Force," which introduced readers to his scale of consciousness. In his book "Letting Go," Dr. Hawkins

talks about the importance of letting go of all feelings and ignoring one's thoughts. He went as far to
state that all our thoughts are merely rationaliza-
tions of our feelings. It is no surprise that Dr. David
Hawkins was one of the early students of Lester
Levenson's Sedona Method.

I had an epiphany upon reading the words of
Dr. Hawkins and realized in that moment that peace
should be a *thoughtless* activity. By this, I mean that
when there is peace, there should not only be no
feelings, but also no thought. One should stop all
thought in the moment of connecting with that
peace within. To the extent that we can get ourselves
to a state of *zero* feelings and zero thoughts, we will
be moving out of the way and letting some higher
power take over to do whatever needs to be done in
our lives. Instead of fighting so hard for or against
certain outcomes through our holding on to positive
or negative emotions, we instead shift into a neutral
state and let the Universe do its job.

The good news is that this profound state of
healing can be effected by you. You do not need
a healer or a third party to do it for you, although
being in the presence of a teacher with an elevated
consciousness can often *reshape your consciousness* as
well. In other words, when you get in touch with
those deep feelings of peace, you not only have the
ability to effect deep changes in your own life, but
also the lives of others as well. This is perhaps what
the ancient spiritual masters meant when they spoke

of gifting this peace to others. They knew deeply that giving this greatest gift would not leave them with nothing, but instead would enrich their lives in unseen ways.

The peace you have within you is truly the greatest gift because not only can it be applied in different ways to change physical matter, it is also infinite. The peace cannot be diminished or depleted in any way. It is omnipresent. Something that is infinite can never be used up in any way.

As we close this chapter, a verse from the Upanishads, ancient Hindu scriptures that are thousands of years old, comes to mind: "From abundance he took abundance, and still abundance remains." Thus, in the same way: From peace, you can give peace, and still peace remains.

CHAPTER SIX

CHANNELING YOUR GREATEST GIFT

Despite the repeated emphasis on inner peace in the scriptures, why do so many people overlook its importance? One main reason is because of how modern humans perceive inner peace. We see it as a consequence rather than the starting point of all magic and manifestations. We see it as the effect, rather than the cause itself. This erroneous understanding has led us further and further away from recognizing the true powers of channeling this inner peace.

After realizing the powers of this greatest gift for myself, I have come to understand that a sense of inner peace is the catalyst for all our manifestations and transformations in the outer world. All forms of healing and change stem from first cultivating that Universal sense of inner peace on the inside. As such, peace is a necessary condition to work miracles in our outer world. The greatest spiritual teachers who walked the earth and performed miracles always had a clear channel of access to that infinite wellspring of inner peace. They knew how to call upon it at will and immerse themselves into a complete state of absolute peace, even when their physical environment was tumultuous.

In order to help you understand what this deep feeling of inner peace is, it is helpful to point out what it is not. A state of inner peace is not the same as a feeling of denial or resignation. It is not a state in which you feel resigned to all the problems in your life and thus feel "peaceful" because you cannot solve them. This is not what a state of peace is about. Some individuals may seem peaceful, accepting and nonresistant on the outside, but their inner states may portray a completely different picture if you somehow managed to have a glimpse into their inner world.

This was me many years ago. On the surface, I was always calm and composed, afraid of showing signs of worry, fear or negativity to spoil my "spiritual truth seeker" image! But the truth is that I was *very* fearful on the inside about things going wrong. I was always very scared about running out of and not having enough money. What I had only managed to do back then was to *appear* peaceful on a physical level, hoping that my physical actions would bring about the results I desired, when in fact my inner state was a complete mess. Therefore, only you will know your true inner state. It is the only thing you have complete control over. Learning how to tend to your inner state will reap the most rewards in your life.

There is a tendency to look at the lives of others while doing this work and point out the various discrepancies as they relate to these spiritual principles, especially in the beginning. For example, my students often tell me, "My friend Jane doesn't seem to be a positive person and yet good things happen to her all the time!" Or "My uncle Eric does not do any of this spiritual stuff you teach, yet he is filthy rich!"

There is very little value in looking at the lives of others and trying to identify what has led to their results. The reason is because we <u>never</u> have a complete understanding of their inner states! At best, all we can observe are merely their physical behaviors, outer actions and habits of speech. I estimate that this accounts for probably 10% or less of the results in their lives. The remaining 90% comes in the form of their inner thoughts, dialog and emotions that are <u>unobservable to the rest of us</u>. It is this unobservable (and often overlooked) portion that <u>makes all the difference</u>. This is also the reason why Abraham-Hicks say it is a good idea to "mind our own business" and "tend to our own vibrations." We know too little about the lives of others to draw any conclusions.

The value of an experienced mentor or coach lies in his ability to uncover the hidden, unconscious beliefs that lead to undesired results in a particular area. This is true for a coach in *any* arena. A successful football coach is one who not only coaches players at a physical level to perform technical moves with precision, but also teaches his players about the inner game of football. He is one who is able to shine a light on the non-physical aspects of the game and teach his players about their strengths and weaknesses. Observe this for yourself in your everyday life. We see many technically competent individuals (even Olympic-level athletes) who have performed poorly as coaches simply because they only coached their players on the outer, technical aspects of a sport.

My point here is that it is difficult to observe whether a person is truly peaceful on the inside. Only the person himself or herself knows. Other than that, only an intuitive person tuning into the energy fields of that person knows. Many spiritual or religious individuals are really not at peace with themselves at all. Although they may appear pious on the outside, they actually live with a deep sense of fear and superstition on the inside. This can be seen at a physical level, when they frequently tell or instruct others on how to behave properly, in line with certain religious standards. These individuals are quick to point out the flaws of others and how they do not fit in with religious teachings. Understand that this is not a true sign of inner peace. When you have achieved total peace, **everything and everyone will be alright to you.** You will be able to look at the actions and behaviors of every individual and feel loving kindness for them, even though you may not personally agree with their actions or choose the same for yourself.

This is what I call the *litmus* test for peace. As I guide you through an exercise to experience this sense of peace, the litmus test for whether you are there yet will be how you feel about the things that normally displease you. Do they feel jarring to you? Do they seem particularly obvious to you? Do you feel a need to open your mouth and say a few words? Do you feel a need to physically intervene? If your answer to any of those questions is "yes," then you have not reached that state of inner peace. When you are *in* peace, you merge with the Universal consciousness. You become one with all that is. In that state, all negative emotions and the need to be right simply melt away.

I encourage you to take dips into this state of inner peace as often as you like. As mentioned, your dips do not have to last long. They can merely be a few seconds. But in those few seconds, you will experience the eternity and entirety of the whole Universe. This is perhaps what English poet William Blake was trying to convey when he said that you can "hold infinity in the palm of your hand and eternity in an hour." The perfection of the whole Universe becomes intuitively known to you in a single dip.

To start, close your eyes and take three deep slow breaths. Breathe in deeply and then out slowly again each time. You do not have to rush any of this. Take as much time as you would like. Let's suppose that you intend to take a dip in the pool on a nice summer day. Would you rush through your morning to take that dip? Probably not. You would do all the things that are necessary, one step at a time. First, you would probably have a nice shower. Next, you would slip into your swimming attire and then you would slowly lower yourself into the water. Similarly, taking three (or more) slow deep breaths and then breathing out serves as a preparation for you to take that relaxing dip. There is no need to rush through any of the preparatory steps.

The purpose of the slow deep breaths is to relax your body physically. Unless your body is physically at ease, it can be difficult to enter into a peaceful inner state. As you become more proficient at these exercises, you will find yourself "leading with your mind" more often. This means that you can get your physical body to feel relaxed at will, simply by holding a light intention for relaxation. But for now, you want to let the body lead the mind. When the body is still, the mind stops being so tense as well.

As you sit in a comfortable position with your eyes closed, adopt an inward focus and turn inward. Contrast this with how you usually operate in the outer world. Normally, when your eyes are closed and when you attempt to meditate, your physical senses are still very alert to input from the outer world. You may hear the drone of your air purifiers, the sound of insects or leaves rustling in the wind. You may become particularly sensitive to how your clothing feels on your skin or how well your back is supported by the seat cushion.

Let all these sensations be there while you adopt an inward focus. In other words, while you notice these outer sensations, now turn inward and use your inner senses to pick up what is happening on the inside. You may get nothing at first, not because nothing is there, but because you have allowed yourself to tune these sensations out in the past. These inner sensations and impulses have become so familiar to you that you have conveniently ignored them. But with this exercise, you are making a conscious decision to be in touch with them once again.

Breathe at a natural rate without trying to control anything at all. In the beginning, you may notice your heartbeat becoming more obvious to you. That's a good sign, because while your heart is pulsing in every moment, you hardly pay attention to it. So now, by closing your eyes and turning inward, you have picked up on the first few physical signs of what is happening in your physical body. Noticing your heartbeat or any bodily sensations is the first step.

What you are doing here is consciously reigning your focus in. At first, all you could pick up were sounds and sensations that were quite far from your physical body (the rustling of the leaves outside). But now, you have tightened your zone of perception to an extremely small physical circle that you perceive things *inside* your body. While this is still part of your physical environment, it is a sign that you are making good progress. According to Seth, our physical bodies and skin form the boundaries between our spiritual and physical world.

Our bodies are literally the barriers between our non-physical and physical worlds. It sometimes helps to use a visual analogy as reference. Picture one of those cross-sectional diagrams of the earth that show a sphere with different layers of the earth's crust down to the very core. Using the same analogy, anything inside the sphere is our inner non-physical world. The outer layer represents our bodies, while anything beyond that represents our outer environment.

What we are attempting here is to move from perceiving the physical world of matter (that outer layer) that we are accustomed to, to the non-physical (spiritual) world of *non-matter*. By noticing your heartbeat and other bodily sensations, you are now at the boundary between your physical world and non-physical world. All you need to do is cross over. However, crossing over means you no longer perceive with your five physical senses. You need to use your sixth intuitive sense in order to do so. I call this process "dropping / dipping into peace."

(Note: Before we proceed further, I recommend that you read my full narrative a few times with eyes open all the way through before setting the book aside and trying out the complete procedure for yourself.)

CHAPTER SEVEN
DROPPING INTO PEACE FOR THE FIRST TIME

Once you are at the peripheral boundary between your outer physical world and inner spiritual world, all it takes is a conscious intention to turn your perception inward. Some readers may feel an acute sense of fear or apprehension at this point because it is something they have never done in their lives. They are so attached to using their physical senses and physical bodies that the thought of turning inward into the void can stir up great feelings of uncertainty and fear in some people. Understand that these feelings are natural. They are part of human nature. At the same time, know that you can use the letting go process to let these feelings of fear go. I cover the letting go process in several of my other books.

This process will be much easier if you have done some kind of inner work (for example, meditation) or followed the techniques in my previous books. If so, then making the transition from observing your physical to your spiritual nature will be effortless. However, if it is the first time you have been exposed to this material, then you might feel a slight sense of apprehension. These feelings arise because you are moving into unchartered territory within. You may have been living in a very outer-directed manner for your entire life, interacting with physical objects and boundaries that are around you. As such, you may be at a loss as to how to navigate your inner world.

Know that these fears are not real and that nothing untoward can happen to you, even if you turn your conscious awareness inward. On the contrary, you're about to discover a beautiful and intricate inner world, filled with exquisite details that you never noticed before. These subtle qualities of your being have always been there since the beginning. But you may have missed them as a result of suppressing your inner nudges in favor of more objective physical evidence. Let everything that happens be okay.

When you are at the periphery between your physical and non-physical world, you have a greater awareness of the physical sensations in your body. For example, you may notice your breathing, your heartbeat or even certain muscles twitching. Let this be a sign that you have narrowed your sphere of focus such that you are now perceiving things that are happening *within* your body. At the same time, make no attempt to control any of those physical sensations. Let everything that happens be alright. Sometimes, you suddenly feel a need to regulate or control your breathing: to make it faster or slower. Let the need to do so go. Let whatever pace of breathing be alright. Your pulse may temporarily quicken when you place your conscious awareness on it. Your heart may even start racing. This is a bio-feedback mechanism where conscious awareness on your heartbeat causes you to place more attention on it, which in turn increases your pulse rate even more. If that's the case, just take a few deep breaths and relax more deeply.

The key to doing these exercises is to remember these two truths. First, you are not rushing to go anywhere, so take as much time as you would like. This means following the steps when you have a block of free time, rather than squeezing it between two appointments. Time pressure is always counterproductive. Second, you are not rushing to achieve anything. There is nothing to be "achieved" in the state of peace. A greater part of your being is eternally connected to that greater Universal peace. All you are doing is reminding your conscious self of this truth.

Take as much time as you need to settle down into a relaxed and peaceful state. You may feel your muscles relaxing or your shoulders drooping slightly. Once you feel truly calm and at ease, when you perceive no need to rush, that is the moment you can **drop into peace.** The dropping process itself is nondescript on the outside but profoundly transformative on the inside. It is not an intellectual process. There are no logical thoughts or steps you have to hold in your mind. If thoughts such as "Am I doing it right?" or "Is this the way I should be feeling?" pop up in your mind, you're trying too hard to intellectualize the process! There is no thought involved when dropping into peace, so let go of any need to rationalize.

We drop into peace with a conscious and light intention to do so. The most effective way for me is to think "peace" and <u>let it happen</u> for me. I phrase the intention as a single word because the shorter the statement, the fewer opportunities there are for my logical brain to draw associations and rationalize. After a while, I do not even have to consciously think "peace." I just feel an inner shift as I settle into a state of complete stillness. In that instant, my being *becomes* like a pendulum at its highest point, absolutely still in time and space, *in* this world and yet not *of* it.

What do you feel in this moment of peace? You will not lose your conscious awareness. In fact, you will still be acutely aware of all the physical stimuli around you. At the same time, you will perceive an inner sense of stillness and notice how vast that stillness is. Perception of this vastness does not come in a form that is recognizable to your five senses. For example, you see an open field and know it spreads over a wide area because of the sensory input from your eyes. But in this case, you perceive the peace as boundless, not because your eyes tell you so, but because your inner senses tell you so. You just intuitively *know* it to be so. This is a perfect example of using your inner senses to perceive the world within you.

You may also feel a buzzing or trembling sensation in your body. These sensations are brought about by an *absence* of motion rather than the presence of them. Your physical body has become so used to being in constant motion that when you become still and silent for one moment, the absence of motion causes an energetic buzz within you.

When I settle into my inner peace, I perceive a sense of being sucked into the center of my body. I do not feel these sensations with my physical senses, but rather, through my inner senses. After some practice, you'll become adept at picking up the impulses sent by your inner senses and contrast them with those sent by your five senses. Accompanying this sense of being sucked into a void at the center of my being is a feeling of physical expansiveness, as if I have just been led through one end of a black hole and emerged from the other end. Picture a V-shaped funnel tapering into black hole with another funnel leading out through the other side. That provides a good pictorial representation of what I mean.

The interesting thing is that I always perceived these sensations even before I read Itzhak Bentov's description of the zero-point pendulum, so his explanation really resonated with me. Whatever the mechanisms are behind the process, you do not have to understand or pinpoint the exact science to experience the same benefits for yourself.

The immediate physical feelings that arise once you have dipped into that inner sense of peace will be a sense of expansiveness and joy. I often break out in goose bumps all over my body. This is also the point at which the Law of Attraction starts to draw good-feeling thoughts into my consciousness.

For example, you may feel your mind drifting off to pleasant memories or thoughts. When you have these thoughts running through your mind, you are strictly speaking, no longer in that state of profound peace, but that's not a bad thing at all! What's more important is that you have dipped yourself in a bit of that peace to begin with.

The state of complete peace is a totally non-resistant and allowing state. That's why when you reach that point, you are in such a state of allowance that good-feeling thoughts and sensations just rush to fill up your beingness. Dipping into that peace, even for extremely short periods at a time, can have far-reaching implications for your wellness and well-being. Even without any conscious attention to the various problems and issues in your life, you may find that these issues subsequently straighten themselves out, as I've discovered for myself. Divine intelligence is present in its purest and most subtle form in this inner peace. This is what quantum physicists refer to as the zero-point field from which an extraordinary amount of energy can be created and directed toward different applications.

Yet there is no need to consciously "direct" this energy with our will. I have found that when we allow ourselves to dip and settle into this peace for even very short periods of time (one to two seconds), we reap all the regenerative and healing benefits of this peaceful potential of energy. It's like returning to the wellspring of Source that gave rise to everything and taking a bath there.

Therefore, do not worry about whether the source energy will know what your problems are and pinpoint them correctly in your life. When you first get yourself to a state of peace, you will be stepping aside and letting divinity do its magic through you. The infinite intelligence of our Universe knows what needs to be done and does it to perfection every single time. It would be a mistake to dip into this peace and then try to turn it into some kind of a manifestation technique. Some people deliberately intend what they want or repeat affirmations when they are at that state of peace. I have found this to be counterproductive and unnecessary. You do not need to tell the Universe what you want in words. The Universe already knows clearly and precisely what you want. When you are at that source of peace, there is no need to justify or keep asking for what you want. There is no need to convince the Universe that you deserve to have what you ask for. All asking is merely unnecessary convincing or persuading. Instead, when you are at *zero*, you <u>allow</u> what you have always asked for to come to you. Thus, the greatest gift of peace is putting yourself into a state of nonresistant allowance to receive what you have always asked for.

There is great value in pausing and getting in touch with this peace during the busy or seemingly tumultuous periods of your life. When the problems of your outer world overwhelm or upset you, it is a good idea to get in touch with this peace at once. When you feel yourself swamped with fears and worries, it is also a good idea to seek this peace out at once. Resist the urge to pick up the phone and talk to someone about your problems! Conventional wisdom tells us that the more we talk about our problems and let off steam, the better we will feel. But I've already shown you that the more you talk about the problem, the more thought energies you focus onto it and hence the more you continue to perpetuate the situation!

Let this be a new way through which you enjoy life. When in doubt or fear, call upon peace. This is what the Bible has always told us to do, although the message may have been lost through the ages and various translations. This peace is always within you, ready to be called upon at the slightest notice.

If you do this unfailingly every single time you meet with an obstacle on the outside, you'll find these obstacles resolving themselves every single time. You'll find yourself led to the right solutions to take, at the right time. When I first started using these techniques of going within, I was faced with several problems in my life that I perceived as stubborn and insurmountable. But I persistently returned to the source of peace each time I felt emotionally overwhelmed. Within a few months, all the perceived issues in my life cleared up and nothing upset me anymore. I still continue to be in touch with my peace for at least once a day.

This fundamental, often overlooked ability to call upon peace at any time has turned out to be my greatest gift. It can be yours too once you call upon it.

CHAPTER EIGHT

TRANSMUTING THE GIFT INTO OUTER MANIFESTATIONS

This deep wellspring of inner peace has been called various names throughout the ages. Quantum scientists call it the zero-point field and the implicate order. Spiritualists call it the Divine or Universal mind, the infinite field of all possibilities. Whatever name we choose to know this infinite potential by does not matter, so feel free to give it any label you like or better still, no labels at all. I prefer to just call it *peace* because that is the name that best resonates for me at this point.

Bringing forth the inner power of peace is not an intellectual process. Give up the need to identify this inner sense of peace or associate it with anything you know from your previous experience. I've found this form of categorization to be too limiting. Whenever we try to label a new experience by associating it with something we know (or read) from the past, we limit the possibilities that can be experienced. The zero-point field is infinite in and of itself. It is everyone and everything at the same time.

It is boundless and timeless. Only by keeping true to its infinite nature can infinite possibilities and outcomes manifest for you. Be open to all the possible paths of unfolding.

The greatest gift of inner peace can be used for many practical applications. I have never been one to shy away from using these spiritual gifts for practical purposes. I have used them to manifest financial abundance, material goods, relationships, health and also wellness in all areas of my being.

The strange thing about using the greatest gift to manifest your heart's desires is that you soon run out of material things to manifest. In the beginning, life becomes an exciting adventure as you experience material wealth beyond your wildest dreams. You realize, perhaps for the first time in your life, that you can truly have everything you dreamed of. But after a series of material manifestations, you start to lose interest in materialistic goods as you realize that the power has always been in you—not in those material items that you associated so much of your well-being and security with previously.

It is strange, but along with a realization of my manifestative abilities, I have lost my desire for luxurious or hedonistic goods of any kind. This does not mean that I am unable to function as a person or appreciate the finer things in life. I still buy expensive items once in a while when they are value for money, but usually for a functional purpose and not for the need to look or feel good. For example, I recently manifested a car (the story is told in my book "Let The Universe Guide You!"). While I could have gone without one, I saw the car as central to fulfilling my higher purpose as a joyful creator, by allowing me to travel physically to various places to seek out new information and experience new things.

The reason why I feel inclined to explain this here is because you may find yourself changing on the inside after learning these manifestation principles. Students are often worried when they find their tastes and preferences changing, often drastically overnight! Some of them are even afraid of losing their minds or that they'll die soon. Please be assured that this is <u>not</u> the case. If anything at all, what is dying will be your old ways of thinking and acting in the world. This marks the start of an awakening to your true nature.

The second group of readers who are worried are those who ask, "Will learning about these manifestation principles cause me to lose all my desires? If so, I would rather not learn them!" This is really a catch-22 situation because you will indeed lose all your desires for materialistic goods if you go far enough down the path. But that is certainly no reason to hold yourself back. Rest assured, you will <u>not</u> lose your ability to enjoy life. Life will become more blissful, peaceful and happier for you. You will have everything you need even without any desire for material wealth and riches. You will still live a rich life beyond your wildest dreams, it's just that you do not have to seek or strive for any of it.

The best analogy I can offer here is this: When you know you have a Universal wellspring (of transmutable energy) to draw upon, then what is left to fear? You'll be self-assured and at peace with everything in your life. You'll know that whenever you have a need to be met, the means to meet that need will also present themselves to you simultaneously. There is no need for worry or fear. From this perspective, there is no need to hoard anything or prove anything to anyone at all. All fear evaporates. There is no need to amass a stash of money or luxury goods just to tell the world that you have made it. When you learn how to tap into the Universal wellspring of peace, you have everything you need at every moment. You had it all along!

One of the early affirmations I learned from Catherine Ponder was, "All my needs are met at every point in time and space." In the early days, I would feel a deep sense of peace wash over me as I read this affirmation to myself on the inside. It brought me great assurance and kept my worrisome thoughts at bay. Then one day after doing all this inner work, I realized, "Holy cow! This has been true all along! How silly I've been all this while, repeating something that is already true!"

I've been reading that affirmation all those years "hoping" it would one day come true for me, not realizing it has always been that way! It has always been true! I was indeed, only affirming the truth for myself. I was the one who needed convincing, not

the Universe! The moment I had this precious realization, I stopped my practice of repeating affirmations over and over again.

I see peace or the zero-point field as giving rise
to the subtlest forms of energy. Energy at this basic
level is pure and formless. It is from this pure state
that energy can be transmuted into various physical
forms in line with our heart's desires. Subtle energy
is light and invisible to our five senses. Therefore, we
do not interact or shape this energy with our hands
as we mold a piece of clay, which is much denser
energy.

The key to transmuting subtle energy is through
the power of our intentions and mental focus.
Again, one can read any text on spiritual healing to
verify this. All forms of spiritual healing tap into a
divine consciousness, a Universal energy field that
is infinitely intelligent. All spiritual healers channel
this divine energy (often by offering themselves as a
conduit) through the use of their undivided focus
and attention to bring forth healing.

While healing is the dissolution of unwanted ill-
nesses and symptoms (unwanted manifestations), a
deliberate manifestation is the opposite. It is the creation of wanted conditions in our lives. Therefore,
there is really not much difference in the dynamics
of the two. It goes without saying that all of these
manifestation steps can also be used to effect spiritual healing.

When most people read about modern day
healing encounters, they often say, "I sure wish I

had this special ability!" I used to say so myself each time I read a book on spiritual healing. "I wish I had his abilities!" Little did I know that this belief was keeping me from performing the same miracles. But believing that I was different or that I did not have these innate abilities, I had limited my possibilities.

The greatest surprise came when I realized that **everyone has those abilities**, myself included! That was a great epiphany. While all of us have these innate abilities, what differs is how we access these latent abilities for ourselves. I reasoned that it wouldn't make sense for these abilities to require an instruction manual to operate, neither would it make sense if we needed a PhD to work them. Their access should hinge on something more fundamental than that, a basic quality that resides in every human being on the planet today.

On the cover of this book, I have chosen an image of three nicely wrapped gifts. Notice how each of these gifts is tied with a beautiful ribbon. To get to the gifts contained within the package, one has to first undo the knot created by the ribbon. This is where an appropriate analogy comes into play: If you had no idea how knots worked, you could tug at the wrong end of the ribbon and make the knot even tighter with each pull. You could find yourself exerting lots of energy while not getting anything done. Over time, the knot would become a dead knot that is impossible to undo without cutting the string.

On the other hand, if you knew which end to pull, the whole knot would come loose with a single, light tug. No effort is needed, just a light pull. This is a useful analogy to keep in mind as you are shaping this subtle energy: No force is needed, just a gentle pull in the right place and the wrapping comes apart. Any time you find yourself using force or straining yourself, you are actually making the knot tighter.

CHAPTER NINE

SHAPING SUBTLE ENERGY FOR OUTER MANIFESTATIONS

We will first talk about how to shape this subtle energy for outer manifestations. There is no need to hold yourself back when directing this subtle energy, as I've found that all concerns about deservingness and appropriateness are self-imposed. As long as you do not direct this energy to harm others (which is impossible and time-wasting since it is loving energy), anything goes. Many students have the concern that they should not ask for too expensive or luxurious things. But as I've mentioned, the Universe does not discern or judge the actual content of your desires, it simply gives you what you are aligned with. **Ask for what you truly want, not for what you think others will judge you by.**

The fundamental basis for any manifestation is to first get yourself into a peaceful state. Follow the instructions in Chapters 6 and 7 to get yourself into a state of deep inner peace while you experience the transcendental nature of that peace. If you stayed there and did nothing else, that would suffice. Recall how I merely accessed this inner peace for brief moments during troubling times, and that was all that was needed to effect changes in my outer situation. Therefore, even if you remained in this pure positive energy and did nothing else, the openness of your being while in this powerful state would create far-reaching changes in your outer reality.

At the level of peace, nothing exists. Because nothing exists in form, *everything* is possible. Remember the earlier saying by Bashar? "When it seems like you have no options, that is when you have an <u>infinite</u> number of options available to you." Remember Bentov's pendulum? While it appears that the pendulum is absolutely still and doing nothing in our physical dimension, it is actually simultaneously present in all dimensions at once. It has become out of this world and yet *in* every world at the same time. The essence of these two narratives (and many others in various religious texts) point to a fundamental point: That by doing nothing and becoming still, one becomes the sum total of everything at a single point in time. This is perhaps the closest I can come to describing this paradox in physical words. You'll have to experience the rest of it for yourself.

If you had an infinite number of options available to you, what would you choose to become? At the energetic level, the question becomes: If you could create anything from this peace, what would you choose to create? The answer, of course, is totally up to you.

Become a pure channel for this peace without altering it in any way. Become a pure channel for this peace without trying to categorize or fit it within the confines of what you already know. This peaceful state is formless and a representation of the infinite possibilities that are to come into your life.

While you are immersed in that peaceful state, you will experience two things. First, you will feel a profound sense of assuredness and security wash over you. You will have a deep inner knowing that everything is alright and has always been, whatever the outer circumstances may be. You will know that no matter what happens, you have the deep inner resources to transcend any obstacles. You'll also know that all obstacles are merely man-made illusions. I experience this as a grounding of my being, as if I am supported by a very firm and solid spiritual foundation. This sensation is further enhanced if I close my eyes while dipping into this inner peace. Second, you will feel a sense of timelessness, as if time and space do not exist at all. You'll feel time coming to a standstill for you, or that you momentarily lose any concerns about physical time.

These should be the two main sensations that you experience while in this profound state of inner peace. If you find your peace disturbed by thoughts of "whether I am doing it right," "whether I am there yet" or even your fears about the process, then you are <u>not</u>

in that state of peace. Let those intruding thoughts go and the whole of your being will get there.

To recap our journey up to this point: We first relax our physical bodies and narrow our zones of physical awareness. Eventually, we switch from using our physical senses to perceiving with our inner senses. Finally, we reach that sacred moment where we drop into peace—where all thinking stops and we get to experience the whole of our being.

Most people logically assume that they'll not be able to function when thought activity ceases. That cannot be further from the truth. The reverse is actually true. When you manage to stop all thoughts (or stop engaging in your thoughts), you experience the fullness of your being and see yourself as who you really are. You begin to perceive that white sheet of paper as it really is, rather than a white sheet of paper covered with scribbles and pen marks. You realize that the black piece of paper you have been staring at all along is actually white! That is the point where your awareness actually grows instead of becoming closed off. Therefore, a sense of awareness does not depend on intellectual activity or thought. You can be extremely aware of everything that is happening and the nature of reality without your usual logical thought activity.

This is also the reason why a state of peace is accompanied by a sense of expansiveness. When you become simultaneously aware of the fullness of your being, you realize that you are not bound by space or time limitations. You can be everywhere across every point in time. Does this sound like Bentov's pendulum again? This is exactly what Bentov was trying to convey. This magical moment is when you gain access, not physical access but <u>spiritual</u> access to *all* worlds and dimensions. This is when you realize the fullness of your connection with the entire Universe.

Visualize the pristine surface of a perfectly calm and still lake. Any pebble that you drop into this lake will produce perfectly formed ripples that radiate outward with maximum amplitude. If you drop several pebbles at once, you'll end up with several interfering wave patterns on the water surface canceling each other out. That's why if your thoughts are scattered, it is unlikely that they will lead to fast and precise outer manifestations. Your thoughts and intentions are canceling each other out! If you drop pebbles into a lake with choppy waters, you will not get well-formed ripples. The choppy waters represent a turbulent inner state filled with negative emotions.

The above analogy illustrates a few important points: First, we must have a completely calm and still lake. We have achieved this by first settling ourselves into a state of profound inner peace. Second, we must drop only one pebble into the water at a time. This means we must control our minds in such a directed and focused way that we eliminate all other pebbles or sources of interference. Note that we are *dropping* a pebble into the water as opposed to throwing it in. The act is as effortless as *dropping* something into the water. No force is needed to hurl anything into the water. We all know that it is futile to use force when trying to create beautiful ripples on the water surface.

Let's translate the above analogy into practical steps. The pebble represents your intention, the very thing that you are trying to manifest. We know that the pebble has to be small to avoid creating a big splash in the water. This means we must use a very direct and laser-focused intention. Let's suppose that you are trying to manifest more money into your life. That by itself is a very loaded topic. When you think about money, many accompanying emotions and topics crop up for you. For example, you may think about money in terms of the debt that you currently owe or in terms of increasing your salary. Money means different things to different people and the concept is so loaded that it is hardly a small pebble!

Therefore, using "I want more money" as an intention will be like trying to drop a big rock that you have to carry with both hands into the water. You will not produce far-reaching ripples but instead a splash with many interfering wave patterns. <u>The trick therefore is to turn your rock into a small stone</u>. Now *that* takes some mental creativity and it is also the reason why most students of manifestation never get to this stage. Manifestation *is* a creative endeavor. You *do* have to exercise your creative faculties a bit here.

By the way, all of this should be done before you enter into a state of inner peace. This means that you should already have decided on the "pebble" you are going to use even before getting into a peaceful state. All of this is preparatory work that you do *before* dipping into the state of inner peace.

One way of turning that big rock into a small round pebble is to focus on a particular aspect of money. For example, what does money mean to you? What does financial abundance mean to you? For some people, even saying "I want to earn $10,000 a month" is a big rock for them, because then they'll start thinking of all the associated "issues" that come with earning that amount of money per month. For example, should I ask for $15,000 or $10,000? Which debt should I settle first when I really make that level of income? Pay attention to the associated thoughts that come up when you think of that intention. If many associated thoughts come up for you, then you have picked a big rock and not a pebble. This means your intention is very loaded and filled with lots of sub-intentions that scatter your energy.

This is also why I encourage people to focus on their **feelings** instead of using words. When we use feelings, we bypass all thoughts and go directly to the feeling. For example, I first close my eyes and identify how it feels like for me to be making $10,000 a month. That feeling carries with it a unique vibrational sensation. It makes me *feel* a certain way on the inside. Really identify and get into the essence of that feeling. Notice how that feeling does not bring up any associated intentions or thoughts for you? Notice how no contradictory thoughts come into your mind when you hold on to that feeling? That's because there are no words for your logical mind to process and chew on! This is the exact reason why spiritual teachers encourage the use of feelings as opposed to words. But one thing to note is that the *feeling* has to be very pure and clear in itself. It cannot be a feeling of financial abundance mixed with some kind of worry. Otherwise, we are back to that "one pebble versus two" issue again. Practice refining your feelings until they are very pure.

The exact same recipe applies for spiritual healing. Whether trying to heal yourself or another person, get in touch with the vibrational essence of how it feels when the person is completely healed. What does it feel like? That feeling *becomes* your pebble that you'll drop into the field of peace. When put this way, we understand that spiritual masters are individuals just like you and me, except that they have a natural (or perhaps trained) ability to feel extremely <u>pure feelings</u> that match their desired end states. The ability to feel extremely pure feelings that match our desired manifestations **is a skill that can be practiced over time.** When you master this skill, you will be able to quickly and effectively manifest anything you want, every single time.

I started out as an extremely poor manifestor because I was not good at channeling my pure feelings. Those feelings I held that I thought were "pure" were actually mixed with all sorts of contradictory vibrations. As a result, the Universe picked up on all of them and gave me contradictory, limited results. The moment I understood the importance of getting in touch with the <u>pure vibrational essence</u> of things, my world changed in an instant. This refinement of feelings is an esoteric practice that many religious sects and traditions guard extremely closely. All of them have come up with different ways for their followers to channel extremely pure feelings (vibrations) through their inner states and therefore achieve certain outcomes. This may be done through the chanting of certain mantras, adoption of certain physical postures or the vocalization of certain frequencies. But understand that you can <u>train yourself</u> to reach this pure feeling state through practice and feedback. This is the probably the first time I am revealing this information in print.

If I wanted to manifest anything, I would probably spend 90% of my time studying how I could become vibrationally pure and in tune with what I wanted to manifest and 10% of my time doing the steps and techniques outlined above. The 90% is crucial to get to that pure feeling state. If your mental energy is even a little bit mixed, then you are going to experience delayed manifestations. Therefore, spend some time looking for creative ways to channel this pure energy within yourself. With practice and successes, you will become very adept at this.

I often find myself being able to get in touch with the pure vibrational essence of my desired manifestations very quickly. For example, let's assume that I am trying to manifest a particular object in my life. How will I feel when that object is mine? I dive deep into the vibrational feelings behind that experience and identify the inner sensations that stand out for me. Next, I test this sensation to see if there are any contradictory vibrations within. This is not an intellectual process and the answers come to you the moment you ask. You'll feel it in your being if there are any contradictory feelings of worry or fear associated with what you are trying to manifest. If there is a presence of contradictory feelings, then you can either find a new way to vibrationally represent what you are trying to manifest or use the letting-go steps that I have written about in my previous books.

The entire key is to drop into a state of inner peace and **at that point of profound stillness**, gently drop the pebble into the water without strain or effort. You do so by bringing to mind the pure vibrational feelings you have identified with earlier at that exact moment. Therefore, if I am intending to help someone heal, I drop into peace and when in that peaceful state effortlessly hold the vibrations of "total and complete healing" on the inside. If I am intending to manifest a particular object, I drop into peace and when in that peaceful state hold the vibrations of my desired manifestation on the inside. You will realize when doing so that you literally become the vibrational essence of what you are trying to manifest. In that moment, you **ARE** abundance. You

ARE joy. You **ARE** whatever it is that you intend to create.

You do not have to hold these feelings for long. How long does the pebble have to stay on the surface of the water in order to create ripples? That would be an absurd question to ask! The pebble does its own thing naturally. The same applies here. How long do you have to hold on to these feelings? The vibrations do their own things naturally in accordance with the laws of the Universe. Therefore you do not have to hold on to these feelings at all. The moment you drop into that state of inner peace and channel that intention within you, **it is done!** The whole affair is complete in less than a second. What it depends on is: (1) the calmness of your inner state and (2) the purity of your directed intentions. IT IS DONE!

CHAPTER TEN

THE NONVERBAL PROTOCOL FOR GIVING THE GIFT

As you become more proficient with these techniques, you'll find yourself doing them both standing up and sitting down. You'll find yourself getting in touch with your inner peace without the need to close your eyes. You'll find yourself dropping into peace while your physical body is in motion, as you are engaged in other life activities.

Again, the idea here is joyful experimentation. Recall the analogy of dropping a pebble or loosening a knot by pulling on the right end of the string. There is no strain or struggle in any of this. Let everything happen naturally. When you have mastered the process sitting down and closing your eyes, you'll find yourself gaining the ability to do it sitting down with your eyes open and so on.

I have been playing with this for such a long time that I can become aware of an issue usually while in conversation with another person. While still talking to them or when they are turned away briefly, I drop into my state of inner peace and <u>simultaneously</u> direct my purest intentions for the resolution of that issue. I do so not because I would like to gain their favor or appear superior, but because I feel genuine compassion for whatever they are going through in life, having gone through the same struggles myself.

Therefore, it does not matter whether what I've done on the inside helps them or not. People often ask, "How do you know what you have done helps them? How do you know you are not fooling yourself?" That's not the point. What I have done has helped me feel better about their situation at the very least. It makes me feel better about what they are going through and changes the way I perceive their situation from one of pity to compassion.

You'll notice how the ego wants to shout out, "I've done it!" after you have done so. You may notice an incredible urge to tell them things like, "I have just cleared things up for you on the inside!" That is nothing more than approval-seeking behavior, which ironically disturbs our inner states even more. You now see why it can be difficult to maintain a calm and peaceful inner state that is conducive for your outer manifestations. Even *after* it is done, your ego wants to tell the world that you have done it! Your ego wants to take credit for what divinity has done. Let those feelings go and be free from them.

There is little value in telling people that you have cleared things up for them on the inside. First, most people will not understand what you're talking about and will look at you as if you have lost your mind. Next, whether you tell them makes no difference to the results and instead creates more mind chatter for you. I often observe that these individual's situations have indeed improved for the better. However, the improvement was certainly not my work. It was the work of the Universe. I merely tapped into this greatest gift within myself, which is also available to everyone else. If they could tap into this gift for themselves, they would rise above their issues as well. It is no coincidence that spiritual healers throughout the ages have asserted the same thing—that a higher power flows and works through the healer. Through the directed use of your pure intentions, you help to effect change in another person by directing the flow of subtle energy. If there is anything else blocking that change, or if that person does not wish for change, your intentions will simply not work. There is no harm in trying.

Now on to the most interesting piece of the puzzle: When you wish to help someone but do not know how to do so, you can always intend "peace" (while being in a state of inner peace) for the other person. That peace will resolve and straighten everything out for that individual. Sometimes I am unable to figure out or get in touch with the pure vibrational energy needed for the resolution of an issue. This happens especially if there are many "issues" in an individual's life and if he has bombarded me with many details, or if I am too emotionally attached to a person. In those situations, I simply intend "peace" and know that divine intelligence will transmute this peace into whatever is needed in his life.

Infinite intelligence knows the path to freedom better than anyone else. I'm having goose bumps now as I write these words because doesn't this remind you of John 14:27? "I'm leaving you at peace. I'm giving you my own peace. I'm not giving it to you as the world gives."

In the context of what we have been discussing, this is a rephrasing of that verse: "Recognizing the power of my inner peace, I am letting this inner peace work for you to resolve everything in your life completely. My definition of peace is not the contrived definition that the world goes by, not in terms of the absence of violence but something deeper than that." Wow!

The most miraculous story of this nonverbal healing power of peace happened to my own mother. Readers of my previous books will know that my mother has been a chronic worrier all her life, always worried about things going wrong and whether she would have enough money for her retirement. Her physical health suffered after she retired, compounded by the lack of a regular income.

I expected my mom to grow increasingly pessimistic and negative as the years went by, and this seemed to be the case for two decades. Her knees were hurting so badly that she could hardly travel. As her son, I felt a strong desire to help her, coupled with a strong sense of emotional attachment to her situation. I knew that getting her to read the books

I had written was not an option because there was no way she was going to accept the ideas presented within, especially if they were from her own son! They were so far from the religious framework and beliefs she had known all her life.

What I instead did was to intend "peace" for her and clear out any blocks for her at a spiritual level, never once telling her what I was doing on the inside. The most miraculous changes occurred. She did not experience spontaneous physical healing but was instead persuaded by a friend to join a gym for weekly exercises. Considering that she had never exercised all her life and hated it, this sudden transformation in her was stunning, to say the least. As she worked out regularly of her own accord, her knee problems corrected themselves and she gained a newfound sense of confidence. Her mood improved, along with a desire to travel to faraway places and experience new things! I've had the pleasure of observing this complete change in her at close range and can tell you that after years of persuasion and emotional blackmailing on my part that did not work, peace finally did it for me.

The most surprising thing was noticing her positive and carefree attitude when we conversed. A few decades of negative thinking had completely disappeared—talk about a quantum shift! I realized that she had somehow <u>intuitively</u> understood most of the spiritual principles I had been trying to convey to her through logical means for the longest time—and she was now repeating them back to me! At that moment, I knew I had to write this book.

You can use the nonverbal protocol to guide the healing power of peace toward someone else. The way to do this is exactly the same as what you would do to apply the technique on yourself. First get in touch with your state of inner peace. When you are at the calmest point, lightly *intend* (in the form of a very direct intention) that healing or improvements occur for a particular person (or group). Remember that you never have to figure out the mundane details of how to help that person. Just intend "peace" for that individual and feel the complete resolution of the issue. Peace is doing the healing and corrections, not you.

Very often, individuals have a strong desire to create improvements in their lives but are blocked by their unconscious beliefs or fears. When you use the nonverbal protocol for peace, you let peace clear some of these blocks in their lives and free up the channels through which the greatest good can flow to them. If they were in a position to apply these techniques for themselves, the same effects would be achieved. Since we are all connected, healing and manifestations can take place across boundaries of time and space. It is possible to use the nonverbal protocol of peace to help other people heal or improve their lives without physically communicating with them. I use the nonverbal protocol on everything and everyone. Children respond particularly well to this protocol because they have relatively few blocks to begin with and may be too young to learn these techniques for themselves.

To allow for the widest possible range of results, it is recommended that you intend "peace" and general improvements for someone and <u>let peace do the work</u> rather than state a very specific outcome. We often do not know what is best for another person. I use a specific intention or outcome only when an individual <u>tells me what he wants</u>. For example, if people express a strong desire to be free from particular physical conditions while conversing with me, I take that as a clear signal of their intention and then intend it for them. Otherwise, I always intend more generally and for a general clearing of the blocks in their lives.

Chapter Eleven

Everyone Has The Capacity For Peace

Many people write to me on a daily basis detailing their issues in life or asking me for ways to help a loved one. I was once such a person, always looking for ways to help others and feeling helpless when I could not. There are only so many people who you can physically help, but the number of people you can touch through your understanding of this sacred peace is unlimited.

No matter what problems you perceive in the lives of others, know these two things: First, that Source (the Universe) does not perceive the same problems as you. And second, when perceptual blocks are corrected, the "problems" dissolve and straighten themselves out as if they were never there in the first place. This is true for any kind of problem in all areas of life.

How does one effect this healing in the first place? The answer, as I've given you throughout this book, is to tap into a fundamental ability that all of us have possessed since the beginning of time. It is the ability to **return to that miraculous state of inner**

peace, a peace so powerful that it can achieve anything. A peace that is not in accordance with how the world perceives it. The moment we do so and get in touch with that transformational state of profound peace, divine intelligence takes over and clears up all the perceived blocks in our lives. It's as simple as that.

There are many people on this planet who have momentarily forgotten how to access this peace for themselves. They have briefly forgotten that this greatest gift lies within them and is not in the hands of anyone else. These are the people who you will most badly want to help because they display the physical symptoms of having forgotten this gift. I have shown you various ways in which you can guide them toward their own greatest peace, as I did for my mother.

Everyone has the capacity for peace. Thus, all you need to do is to guide them toward this peace and let them experience the revitalizing energies for themselves. One often overlooked way for doing so is through the power of your spoken words. The direct verbal method is one of the most effective ways of guiding someone to and helping them experience their inner peace, even for just a little while. It also requires no spiritual background on the recipient's part. This is how the greatest gift was first awakened in me. I had read the words of Seth and heard the soothing words of my mother. Those words led me to a temporary state of profound inner peace and was all that was needed to sort the situation out.

A way to guide people to peace would be to offer encouraging and uplifting words to those around you whenever you can. Don't just offer empty words of encouragement. Give them a genuine piece of your inner peace. Lead them to their own inner peace. When my mother said those words to me many years ago, she really meant them because she believed in me as her son. When Seth wrote those words many years ago for the rest of us, they knew, in their infinite wisdom, that those words would bring profound peace to many of us. In the same way, seek to leave this peace with others in your daily life, no matter what the setting may be. You can give peace in the boardroom or the classroom, on Wall Street or Main Street. You can give peace wherever you are through small gestures and words that help others experience this peace for themselves.

I have experienced the immense satisfaction of leaving my peace with others in various unexpected situations. Take time to hear strangers out in queues and then offer a few divinely inspired words. You'll see their eyes light up once they connect with some of their peace within. You know they long for their issues to be resolved since they are willing to talk about them, so help them clear up some of their blocks along the way in whatever way you can. I do whatever I can to give some peace whether through my verbal words or nonverbal actions, in the same way I was given some priceless peace many years ago that set me on this path. You never know what your gift of peace can eventually lead to.

Seek to give some peace each day of your life to at least one other person. You do not have to be physically near a person to do so. You can give peace to anyone from the comfort of your living room, even to people who have upset you in the past. Always ask yourself, "How can I bring some peace to this situation?" The right words to say or the right actions to take will come to you. At other times, you may feel inspired to use the nonverbal method of giving peace. This is a fundamental ability that you have, so use it for the greatest good!

As you experience the transformational power of peace in your life and in the lives of those around you, you'll understand why peace is really your greatest gift. This peace is not just a mere good feeling on the inside. It can be transmuted through your intentions into love, abundance, health, relationships, bliss, joy and all else that you desire on the outside.

While I may not know what you want in life or the solution to your current challenges, peace knows the way perfectly and can lead you there in divine order. Let peace do the work for you. When in doubt or fear, call upon peace. This peace never fails you nor leaves you, although you may sometimes forget about its existence in trying times. It is omnipotent and omnipresent. It is truly your greatest gift that unlocks all manifestations.

May you always recognize this divine peace within you and allow it to flow abundantly into your life as riches, happiness, wellness and bliss.

May peace be with you, and may you always be at peace.

About The Author

Richard Dotts is a modern-day spiritual explorer. An avid student of ancient and modern spiritual practices, Richard shares how to apply these timeless principles in our daily lives. For more than a decade, he has experimented with these techniques himself, studying why they work and separating the science from the superstition. In the process, he has created successful careers as an entrepreneur, business owner, author and teacher.

Leading a spiritual life does not mean walking away from your current life and giving up everything you have. The core of his teachings is that you can lead a spiritual and magical life starting right now, from where you are, in whatever field you are in.

You can make a unique contribution to the world, because you are blessed with the abilities of a true creator. By learning how to shape the energy around you, your life can change in an instant, if you allow it to!

Richard is the author of more than 20 Amazon bestsellers on the science of manifestation and reality creation. A list of his current books can be found on Amazon at http://amazon.com/author/richarddotts.

AN INTRODUCTION TO THE MANIFESTATIONS APPROACH OF RICHARD DOTTS

Even after writing more than 20 Amazon bestsellers on the subject of creative manifestations and leading a fulfilling life, Richard Dotts considers himself to be more of an adventurous spiritual explorer than a spiritual teacher or "master", as some of his readers have called him by.

"When you apply these spiritual principles in your own life, you will realize that everyone is a master, with no exceptions. Everyone has the power to design and create his own life on his own terms," says Richard.

"Therefore, there is no need to give up your power by going through an intermediary or any spiritual medium. Each time you buy into the belief that your good can only come through a certain teacher or a certain channel... you give up the precious opportunity to realize your own good. My best teachers were those who helped me recognize the innate power within myself, and kept the faith for me even when I could not see this spiritual truth for myself."

Due to his over-questioning and skeptical nature (unaided by the education which he received over the years), Richard struggled with the application of these spiritual principles in his early years.

After reading thousands of books on related subjects and learning about hundreds of different spiritual traditions with little success, Richard realized there was still one place left unexplored.

It was a place that he was the most afraid to look at: **his inner state.**

Richard realized that while he had been applying these Universal principles and techniques dutifully on the outside, his inner state remained tumultuous the whole time. Despite being well-versed in these spiritual principles, he was constantly plagued with negative feelings of worry, fear, disappointment, blame, resentment and guilt on the inside during his waking hours. These negative feelings and thoughts drained him of much of his energy and well-being.

It occurred to him that unless he was free from these negative feelings and habitual patterns of thought, any outer techniques he tried would not work. That was when he achieved his first spiritual breakthrough and saw improvements in his outer reality.

Taking A Light Touch

The crux of Richard's teachings is that one has to do the inner work first by tending to our own inner states. No one else, not even a powerful spiritual master, can do this for us. Once we have restored our inner state to a place of *zero*, a place of profound calmness and peace... that is when miracles can happen. Any subsequent intention that is held with <u>a light touch</u> in our inner consciousness quickly becomes manifest in our outer reality.

Through his books and teachings, Richard continually emphasizes the importance of taking a light touch. This means adopting a carefree, playful and detached attitude when working with these Universal Laws.

"Whenever we become forceful or desperate in asking for what we want, we invariably delay or withhold our own good. This is because we start to feel even more negative feelings of desperation and worry, which cloud our inner states further and prevent us from receiving what we truly want."

To share these realizations with others, Richard has written a series of books on various aspects of these manifestation principles and Universal Laws. Each of his books touches on a different piece of the manifestation puzzle that he has struggled with in the past.

For example, there are certain books that guide readers through the letting-go of negative feelings and the dropping of negative beliefs. There are books that talk about how to deal with self-doubt and a lack of faith in the application of these spiritual principles. Yet other books offer specific techniques for holding focused intentions in our inner consciousness. A couple of books deal with advanced topics such as nonverbal protocols for the manifestation process.

Richard's main goal is to break down the mysterious and vast subject of spiritual manifestations into easy to understand pieces for the modern reader. While he did not invent these Universal Laws and is certainly not the first to write about them, Richard's insights are valuable in showing readers how to easily apply these spiritual principles despite leading modern and hectic lifestyles. Thus, a busy mother of three or the CEO of a large corporation can just as easily access these timeless spiritual truths through Richard's works, as an ancient ascetic who lived quietly by himself.

It is Richard's intention to show readers that miracles are still possible in our modern world. When you experience the transformational power of these teachings for yourself, you stop seeing them as unexpected miracles and start seeing them as part of your everyday reality.

Do I have to read every book in order to create my own manifestation miracles?

Because Richard is unbounded by any spiritual or religious tradition, his work is continuously evolving based on a fine-tuning of his own personal experiences. He does, however, draw his inspiration from a broad range of teachings. Richard writes for the primary purpose of sharing his own realizations and not for any commercial interest, which is why he has shied away from the publicity that typically comes with being a bestselling author.

All of his books have achieved Amazon bestseller status with no marketing efforts or publicity, a testament to the effectiveness of his methods. An affiliation with a publishing house could mean a pressure to write books on certain popular subjects, or a need to censor the more esoteric and non-traditional aspects of his writing. Therefore, Richard has taken great steps to ensure his freedom as a writer. It is this freedom that keeps him prolific.

One of Richard's aims is to help readers apply these principles in their lives with minimal struggle or strain, which is why he has offered in-depth guidance on many related subjects. Richard himself has maintained that there is no need to read each and every single one of his books. Instead, one should just narrow in to the particular aspects that they are struggling with.

As he explains in his own words, "You can read just one book and completely change your life on the basis of that book if you internalized its teachings. You can do this not only with my books, but also with the books of any other author."

"For me, the journey took a little longer. One book could not do it for me. I struggled to overcome years of negative programming and critical self-talk, so much so that reading thousands of books did not help me as well. But after I reached that critical tipping point, when I finally 'got it', then I started to get everything. The first book, the tenth book, the hundredth book I read all started to make sense. I could pick up any book I read in the past and intuitively understand the spiritual essence of what the author was saying. But till I reached that point of understand within myself, I could not do so."

Therefore, one only needs to read as many books as necessary to achieve a true understanding on the inside. Beyond that, any reading is for one's personal enjoyment and for a fine-tuning of the process.

Which book should I start with?

There is no prescribed reading order. Start with the book that most appeals to you or the one that you feel most inspired to read. Each Richard Dotts book is self-contained and is written such that the reader can instantly benefit from the teachings within, no matter which stage of life they are at. If any prerequisite or background knowledge is needed, Richard will suggest additional resources within the text.

OTHER BOOKS
BY RICHARD DOTTS

Many of these titles are progressively offered in various formats (both in hard copy and for the Amazon Kindle). Our intention is to eventually make all these titles available in hard copy format.

Please visit http://amazon.com/author/richard dotts for the latest titles and availability.

- **Banned Manifestation Secrets**

  It all starts here! In this book, Richard lays out the fundamental principles of spiritual manifestations and explains common misconceptions about the "Law of Attraction." This is also the book where Richard first talks about the importance of one's inner state in creating outer manifestations.

- **Come and Sit With Me (Book 1): How to Desire Nothing and Manifest Everything**

  If you had one afternoon with Richard Dotts, what questions would you ask him about manifesting your desires and the creative process? In Come and Sit With Me, Richard candidly answers some of the most pressing questions that have been asked by his readers. Written in a free-flowing and conversational format, Richard addresses some of the most relevant issues related to manifestations and the application of these spiritual principles in our daily lives. Rather than shying away from tough questions about the manifestation process, Richard dives into them head-on and shows the readers practical ways in which they can use to avoid common manifestation pitfalls.

- **The Magic Feeling Which Creates Instant Manifestations**

  Is there really a "magic feeling", an inner state of mind that results in almost instant manifestations? Can someone live in a perpetual state of grace, and have good things and all your deepest desires come true spontaneously without any "effort" on your part? In this book, Richard talks about why the most effective part of visualizations lies in the *feelings*... and how to get in touch with this magic feeling.

- **Playing In Time And Space: The Miracle of Inspired Manifestations**

  In Playing In Time And Space, Richard Dotts shares the secrets to creating our own physical reality from our current human perspectives. Instead of seeing the physical laws of space and time as restricting us, Richard shares how anyone can transcend these perceived limitations of space and time by changing their thinking, and manifest right from where they are.

- **Allowing Divine Intervention**
  Everyone talks about wanting to live a life of magic and miracles, but what does a miracle really look like? Do miracles only happen to certain spiritual people, or at certain points in our lives (for example, at our most desperate)? Is it possible to lead an everyday life filled with magic, miracles and joy?

  In Allowing Divine Intervention, Richard explains how miracles and divine interventions are not reserved for the select few, but can instead be experienced by anyone willing to change their current perceptions of reality.

- **It is Done! The Final Step To Instant Manifestations**
  The first time Richard Dotts learnt about the significance of the word "Amen" frequently used in prayers… goosebumps welled up all over his body and everything clicked in place for him. Suddenly, everything he had learnt up to that point about manifestations made complete sense.

  In It Is Done!, Richard Dotts explores the hidden significance behind these three simple words in the English language. Three words, when strung together and used in the right fashion, holds the keys to amazingly accurate and speedy manifestations.

- **Banned Money Secrets**
  In Banned Money Secrets of the Hidden Rich, Richard explains how there is a group of

individuals in our midst, coming from almost every walk of life, who have developed a special relationship with money. These are the individuals for whom money seems to flow easily at will, which has allowed them to live exceedingly creative and fulfilled lives unlimited by money. More surprisingly, Richard discovered that there is not a single common characteristic that unites the "hidden rich" except for their unique ability to focus intently on their desires to the exclusion of everything else. Some of the "hidden rich" are the most successful multi-millionaires and billionaires of our time, making immense contributions in almost every field.

Richard teaches using his own life examples that the only true, lasting source of abundance comes from behaving like one of the hidden rich, and from developing an extremely conducive inner state that allows financial abundance to easily flow into your life.

- **The 95-5 Code: for Activating the Law of Attraction**
Most books and courses on the Law of Attraction teach various outer-directed techniques one can use to manifest their desires. All is well and good, but an important question remains unanswered: What do you do during the remainder of your time when you are not actively using these manifestation techniques? How do you live? What do you do with the 95% of your day, the majority of your waking hours when you are not actively

asking for what you want? Is the "rest of your day" important to the manifestation process?

It turns out that what you do during the 95% of your time, the time NOT spent visualizing or affirming, makes all of the difference.

In The 95-5 Code for activating the Law of Attraction, Richard Dotts explains why the way you act (and feel) during the majority of your waking hours makes all the difference to your manifestation end results.

- **Inner Confirmation for Outer Manifestations**
  How do you know if things are on their way after you have asked for them? What should you do after using a particular manifestation technique? What does evidence of your impending manifestations feel like?

  You may not have seen yourself as a particularly spiritual or intuitive person, much less an energy reader... but join Richard Dotts as he explains in Inner Confirmation for Outer Manifestations how everyone can easily perceive the energy fields around them.

- **Mastering the Manifestation Paradox**
  The Manifestation Paradox is an inner riddle that quickly becomes apparent to anyone who has been exposed to modern day Law of Attraction and manifestation teachings. It is an inner state that seems to be contradictory to the person practicing it, yet one that is associated with inevitably fast physical manifestations — that of

wanting something and yet at the same time *not wanting* it.

Richard Dotts explains why the speed and timing of our manifestations depends largely on our mastery of the Manifestation Paradox. Through achieving a deeper understanding of this paradox, we can consciously and deliberately move all our desires (even those we have been struggling with) to a "sweet spot" where physical manifestations *have to occur* very quickly for us instead of having our manifestations happen "by default."

- **Today I Am Free: Manifesting Through Deep Inner Changes**

  In Today I Am Free, Richard Dotts returns with yet another illuminating discussion of these timeless Universal Laws and spiritual manifestation principles. While his previous works focused on letting go of the worry and fear feelings that prevent our manifestations from happening in our lives, Today I Am Free focuses on a seldom discussed aspect of our lives that can affect our manifestations in a big way: namely our interaction with others and the judgments, opinions and perceptions that other people may hold of us. Richard Dotts shows readers simple ways in which they can overcome their constant feelings of fear and self-consciousness to be truly free.

- **Dollars Flow To Me Easily**

  Is it possible to read and relax your way into financial abundance? Can dollars flow to you even if you just sat quietly in your favorite arm-chair and did "nothing"? Is abundance and prosperity really our natural birthright, as claimed by so many spiritual masters and authors throughout the ages?

Dollars Flow To Me Easily takes an alternative approach to answering these questions. Instead of guiding the reader through a series of exercises to "feel as if" they are already rich, Richard draws on the power of words and our highest intentions to dissolve negative feelings and misconceptions that block us from manifesting greater financial abundance in our lives.

- **Light Touch Manifestations: How To Shape The Energy Field To Attract What You Want**
  Richard covers the entire manifestation sequence in detail, showing exactly how our beliefs and innermost thoughts can lead to concrete, outer manifestations. As part of his approach of taking a light touch, Richard shows readers how to handle each component of the manifestation sequence and tweak it to produce fast, effective manifestations in our daily lives.

- **Infinite Manifestations: The Power of Stopping at Nothing**
  In Infinite Manifestations, Richard shares a practical, step-by-step method for erasing the unconscious memories and blocks that hold our manifestations back. The Infinite Release technique, "revealed" to Richard by the Universe, is a quick and easy way to let go of any unconscious

memories, blocks and resistances that may prevent our highest good from coming to us. When we invoke the Infinite Release process, we are no longer doing it alone. Instead, we step out of the way, letting go and letting God. We let Universal Intelligence decide how our inner resistances and blocks should be dissolved. All we need to do is to intend that we are clear from these blocks that hold us back. Once the Infinite Release process is invoked, it is done!

- **Let The Universe Lead You!**

  Imagine what your life would be like if you could simply hold an intention for something... and then be led clearly and precisely, every single time, to the fulfilment of your deepest desires. No more wondering about whether you are on the "right" path or making the "right" moves. No more second-guessing yourself or acting out of desperation — You simply set an intention and allow the Universe to lead you to it effortlessly!

- **Manifestation Pathways: Letting Your Good Be There... When You Get There!**

  Imagine having a desire for something and then immediately intuiting (knowing) what the path of least resistance should be for that desire. When you allow the Universe to lead you in this manner and unfold the manifestation pathway of least resistance to you, then life becomes as effortless as knowing what you want, planting it in your future reality and letting your good be there when you get there... every single time! This book shows you the practical techniques to make it happen in your life.

- **And more...**

83892076R00064

Made in the USA
San Bernardino, CA
01 August 2018